nowhere

Mary Burritt Christiansen Poetry Series
Hilda Raz, Series Editor

Mary Burritt
Christiansen
Poetry Series

The Mary Burritt Christiansen Poetry Series
publishes two to four books a year that engage
and give voice to the realities of living, working,
and experiencing the West and the Border as
places and as metaphors. The purpose of the
series is to expand access to, and the audience
for, quality poetry, both single volumes and anthologies, that
can be used for general reading as well as in classrooms.

Also available in the Mary Burritt Christiansen Poetry Series:

origin story: poems by Gary Jackson
Ancestral Demon of a Grieving Bride: Poems by Sy Hoahwah
The Definition of Empty: Poems by Bill O'Neill
Feel Puma: Poems by Ray Gonzalez
Grief Land: Poems by Carrie Shipers
The Shadowgraph: Poems by James Cihlar
Crosscut: Poems by Sean Prentiss
The Music of Her Rivers: Poems by Renny Golden
to cleave: poems by Barbara Rockman
After Party: Poems by Noah Blaustein

For additional titles in the Mary Burritt Christiansen Poetry Series,
please visit unmpress.com.

nowhere

poems

KATIE SCHMID

University of New Mexico Press | Albuquerque

ISBN 978-0-8263-6307-7 (paper)
ISBN 978-0-8263-6308-4 (e-book)

Library of Congress Control Number: 2021937814

Founded in 1889, the University of New Mexico sits on the traditional homelands of the Pueblo of Sandia. The original peoples of New Mexico Pueblo, Navajo, and Apache since time immemorial have deep connections to the land and have made significant contributions to the broader community statewide. We honor the land itself and those who remain stewards of this land throughout the generations and also acknowledge our committed relationship to Indigenous peoples. We gratefully recognize our history.

Cover photograph: adapted from photograph by
fotografierende on Unsplash
Designed by Felicia Cedillos
Composed in ITC New Baskerville 11/14

contents

one

two

three

one

Where is our body?

—SELAH SATERSTROM, *Ideal Suggestions:
Essays in Divinatory Poetics*

Courtship

From the beginning I confused
desire with pain

What is love if not giving someone the power
to make the killing blow

I welcomed the pain
It gave me borders, something to slump against in defeat,
in languor, as I tell you how I'm going to touch you

and I'm going to touch you

just as soon as I finish telling you
how I've been hurt
how I would like you to hurt me

The gulf between my body and yours will always
be a wound

I thought this was an objective fact
true for all the million unloved hordes
until I realized it was a truth formed from
what is called a "childhood"

It suited your purposes
to call me fatherless

and you know that old saw about fatherless girls
and what we would do

There are many things that I would do

as the following PowerPoint outlines

Loving an Addict

Crows crowd the bones
of an oak

A disemboweled car
innard of battery smeared on the asphalt

The remnants of winter
creamed into a grey paste

I wait for a sign in an Olive Garden
off the highway

Winter's art is fatigue unto death

And the smiling knife
of his voice as he lies

On Graduation Night, My Best Friend and I Are in Separate Rooms, Pinned by Our Desire

Here I am lolling like a Millais
against the tiles of the shower,

just graduated, and my boyfriend
shaves my pussy while I drink

champagne—this is how you celebrate,
clap your hands for hairlessness, for being

tended to like a girl prophet, for being
scrubbed like a raw pink pig and taken

to his bed and spread. It was his present.
Hard to stay present, cloud fizz,

champagne fizz. I was a present.
Why didn't I go back to our room

with her, why of all the ways
I could have celebrated, why

choose stupefaction and men, again?
Vapor of diminishing girlhood lifting

out of my folds. Miracle of vapors.
Her face known to me. Loved.

While our separate twinned oblivions
spun into the future. *Were* the future.

Prophecy. A man played her out
of her clothes. Kissed her.

Elsewhere, I spread on the bed.

Prophesy to me, girl goddess
calling to me from the past.

Tell me of our inevitable losing
of one another. As the night

goes, so the rest of our lives.
What if on the path we had not parted.

If I had not walked away from her
toward some lesser man. If I had not

sighed my pink unspeaking mouth
into his mouth and fallen asleep into my future.

At their first meeting, my first boyfriend asks my father, "So, what was prison like?"

When my boyfriend touches me
I feel the wings of my pussy flutter

in time with my breath—I kneel
between his legs in his laundry room

while his mother drinks white wine
in the living room and feel myself

holy when I am so wholly for his pleasure—
This is a love story about my boyfriend's

laundry room and my Laundromat,
the SUV his parents buy him and my mom's

Toyota Tercel with the headlight duct-taped on
like a punched eye—I am giving myself to him

because he has everything, and people
who have everything should have more,

and all the ways I have been told my milk-white
body is a most divine present, all the ways

I think I am made in his hunger,
what his eyes do as they track my body—
I am calling it love—

I am watching him play the piano for hours
and calling it love—

I tell him everything—I watch him—Everything—
I fill my eyes up, plush white carpet in the den—

I know I am placing my neck between the teeth
of a benevolent animal—

At dinner I shyly present the boy
to be viewed in the gloom of my regard—

I am giving him my father, greatest love, greatest
wound—He is shaking his hand—

The boy's teeth elongate at the scent of blood—
I place the points of the animal's teeth just

touching the flesh of my father's neck—

Are you paying attention?

I am giving the animal my father—

All My Boyfriends Love
My Father the Best

He comes to pick me up on his Harley he shows up
with his earring and his jean jacket and my boyfriends

sigh like they want a boyfriend too
he's blaring Led Zeppelin and smoking

a Marlboro and pretending he likes them
as much as me asking who they're reading

oh yeah, he's the shit my Dad says and my boyfriends
go a little weak in the knees—*tell me again* they say

what he did time for? an ex con who reads who listens
to Marley and drinks coffee like a grad student

whose hands are calloused from some romantic labor
and all those tattoos—I can see them squinting

when they look at him, imagining he's Kerouac—
he's everything

they ever dreamed and a Jungian too—and I know
that love where you try so hard to get someone

to see you and it feels like you'll never be let in
to the mysterious house that you know from distant

observation is the most beautiful house, that you know
from closest study   everything
but what it's like to step inside

Health

I thought I could never forgive
my father for how I sat vigil

for the candle of his body.
But there was nowhere else

I would have rather been,
cupping the flame in my child hands.

If he could not tend it
I would tend it.

———

My father told me he could get his brother clean
if only he could lock him

in the basement and separate him
from the world. Like the world

was an animal predator, breath humid,
breath rotten, breath steaming at the seam

of the door.

———

To watch a man with his head cocked,
listening at a door. Who strains to hear

an animal cry heard only by him.

Most beautiful song.

And then to watch him step away
from the thing he seems to love most.

To watch him step back toward you.

Curse

I can't forgive
the men who make me
watch them die

I'm going
to crawl inside their bodies
and wear them

Some Boys of the Midwest

after Ben Marcus

Some boys of the Midwest grow up dirty, covered in earth
like recently dug up root vegetables. They don't have eyes
until they reach twelve years of age, and even so they run
the cul-de-sacs of their neighborhoods in groups of twenty
like blind puppies. They are covered in hundreds of fine
cilia. Their boyhood is porous and lunglike, branched and
gooey, tender to the touch. On weekends after church they
disappear into uncultivated strips of prairie to tend their
silent wounds. To inflict still more wounds upon each other.
They call this happiness. At dusk they file back home to
their mothers' Cloroxed hands, their fathers' too-small polo
shirts. The charcoal briquettes are ashy gray in the grill, and
the trampoline is the most treacherous fun their homes
are capable of. So they fling themselves onto it, again and
again, until they have forgotten what it means to be a boy.
And again, until they are winged creatures. And still more,
until they are planets in space. The lucky ones hang there,
in orbit. The unlucky ones must always come back down for
dinner and submit themselves to questioning. They call this
another kind of happiness.

Some Boys of the Midwest

after Ben Marcus

Some boys prefer to move about the house underneath
the carpets. They move as fluid, furry mounds. They call
this mode of transportation the Rug Node. It is a form of
protection, though it is not without its own kind of danger.
On chore days their mothers' Cloroxed hands push the
vacuum cleaner through the house. Some boys tell a story
of a boy who got caught by the vacuum as he ran his circuit
on the Rug Node. His delicate fur came off first, then his
cilia, then his flesh like fine wet silk. How was the mother
supposed to know, her boy a warm secret under the rug.
The boys tell this story each year in a secret meeting out in
the strip of prairie behind the golf course. It is a cautionary
tale, complete with ritual weeping. Secretly, some have lost
faith that the story is true. An alternate story springs up, in
whispers, with a happy ending. In it, the mother's hands
come upon the true, uncarpeted boy just in time. In it,
the mother discovers her hands had forgotten to turn the
vacuum on all along. That her hands led the mute vacuum
through the house silently. The boys call this a great joke.
The two factions of boys, the believers and the unbelievers,
become contentious. They take to the prairie with sticks to
decide, once and for all, which story is true.

Some Boys of the Midwest

after Ben Marcus

One day, some boys pick a boy whose ribs smile prettily from beneath his skin. They feed him ants, one earwig, a slug. This boy is hugged until he glows with health. He is now their king.

Some Boys of the Midwest

after Ben Marcus

After a long day of school, some boys of the Midwest retire
to the strip of prairie to yell swears. They take off their shirts
and walk into the waist-high grass, grab handfuls of whatever
barbed plant they can find, and chew great mouthfuls of
them until the plants become milk in their mouths. Whoever
blooms with disease first wins. Then they form factions and
curse each other out. They say all the bad words they've
ever known and invent worse names. Eventually a boy
begins to cry from sickness, and they crowd around him,
gather him into their arms, and carry him home. The sick
one is delivered to the father, who sits obscured in a great
mountain of pristine papers. The sick one is crying, and the
father is scared. The father slaps him. This boy has won the
game.

At the Bus Stop

A girl is trying to climb into another girl
through her mouth. They shiver together,
taking up as little space as two girls
can—and slow, through rhythmic
movements of the hips, they try
to find the seam of the world.
They are trying to get out and enter
another world of their own making.
They will go or they will come apart under
each other's hands. Sometimes it feels
like I have been waiting thirty-one years
for someone to touch me the right way,
the way that will make me cease to be
one unbroken stream of longing flooding
the nothing-vessel of my self. I know how
to make myself so you will have to touch me.
I feel her in me. I know I am your girl
the way you always imagined me. The good,
terrible things I know I do to you. I do.
For a little while, I do. Here is the grief
at the heart of my language. Here is the nothing
it seeks to bring into submission.
(How song will sometimes make the scab
you need to live, how touching is a way
of describing what you cannot have, until
it seems every way I lick you births
a new word, and you are newborn,
barely able to stand. My gift, my wound,
where nothing is enough.)

What it's like to never touch the girl you've been longing to touch

I crossed accidentally into the country of never touching her
last night, a nighttime traveler, & I will have to learn
a language I never wanted to know

let's have a moment of silence   for my silence
        for never telling her
        for the inability of language to fit the spaces I need it to

extend the metaphor forever   bring in the strings,
we're going to be here for a while, I am not done
speaking about what I needed to do to her, settle in,
I've been wanting to smear my body with jam

and let the bees carpet me, I've been wanting to smear
my body like jam across the sentence of my disappearance
and make you eat it

Do you hear me, reader, sweet one? Little infinite horse?
Little stinging anemone? There is no language
for the shape of it; it never existed outside of my head—
one night I let its possibility perfume the back seat of a car

and allowed myself to imagine it, spinning it out
like cotton candy. The night pressed its alien starry face
against the car window & watched me invent the country of us
& I had her for a half hour & we flared—

another sun in the back seat—
& I held her & then I killed her & ate the dream.

Crown of Eyes

Because I survived, it became a story
I owed to anyone who asked.

In the telling, I felt eyes rise to the surface
of my skin like goosebumps,

and I gathered them and wore them
as a crown. In the telling,

his hand in mine and the ghost
of his hand in mine, six years

of frisking, of visiting rooms,
of family picnics on Father's Day,

pen full of dads and their children,
lunatic with hunger pangs. Crown

of my aunts' eyes necklacing my head.
All the vending-machine money

I could want. Leaving the visiting
room, the lifeboat of my little

soul floating away from my
drowned father. The guards

and their crown of eyes.

When he Got Out he held my hand on the couch,
and we listened to the Cranberries

and we avoided it,
sitting at the center of us,
and it almost felt like we could fill it with tears,

glittering crown of eyes.

Even after he Got Out I couldn't stop
hunting him. I slept in his shirts,

smelling of his coffee, his cigarettes—
and clutched his phantom fatherbody against mine,

six years of his hand in mine then the ghost
of his hand in mine, and his hand in mine

and the ghost of his hand in mine
for all my life afterward,

and confusing the ghost and the real,
loving the ghost as much as the real,

the facsimile ghost as the father,
the father as the father and *what*

is this ardent night that comes for me?
I am ill, I am faithful always, I will wife it.

two

The scar is a delicate surprise, like sitting alone by a quiet lake at midnight & having the mysterious women step into sight carrying a silver tray with a slice of heat lightning on it . . .

—JEFFREY MILLER

Daughter Psalms

Our fathers
are all brokenhearted, but they still name
every bird, begging us to look at the crows
who scratch and gleam in the dirt.
They name the dark things for us.
In the parking lot alone at night I saw two crows
slow-rise glossy out of the bed of a truck, hover,
and dissolve back into the night.
The two remaining crows shone like black holes
in the bed of the truck. The two last only birds
stared at me, unfriendly, and I thought
of our father who loved them.

blue bird motel

Sisters, it's true: our father has brokenhearted
us. We know the omens: the Blue Bird Motel,
our father sleeping in the middle
of the day. His abandoned body, his blister of a father body.
Let us not love a man who forgets himself so, who abandons
his body in sleep and sleeps with such hunger.
Maybe he never thought to be a father:
his motorcycles, his reckless
burning as a boy, those tattoos. But we love him

in the blood

He gets on his motorcycle and seeks out things to slow
his blood and stop his brain. All manner of things.
All manner of things, alone in a bar or the house of
some other sickened father.

warp

Daughters go to sleep in their fathers'
work suits, the suits smelling of tobacco
and Tic Tacs. In their sleep they cry
for the missing fathers, and neckties orbit
their girl throats as if pacing their skin
in worry. In the morning their humid grief
has warped the floor: the boards rise
in waves.

the hunt

A pack of wild fathers
combs the mountain
at night crying like children.
Many daughters gather for the hunt.
They lie in the grass
with nets and throwing stars.
They pierce the predators
who want the fathers for themselves.
They lie in wait for the fathers,
grief-roaming, until one breaks
from the pack.
A lone father
is easier to catch.
A lone father wants
a daughter to find him.

white horse and the moon

They got to the campsite late, and the father had to set up
in the dark.
His daughter slept in the car, her mouth open
as if about to sing.
The horses came, escaped from their fences. They ran,
strong & trembling
through the camp, so close to the father. In the night,
the white horse began to glow.
Look, said the father, who fetched his sleepy daughter
from the car.
And she stared at her unafraid father and his happiness,
which hung like a moon.

coin

Making a father laugh is like rolling up your pants and
collecting coins from the stream under the bridge. Wade
into the water, which makes your shins cold. Collect the
new, clean money into your wet pockets. There is sun on
your back and a father works beside you, wonders about the
small-time crooks who dumped the change there after a gas-
station heist. The sun is making you sweat, and the father
takes your hand to help you up the muddy bank.

icicles

A father has taken his young daughter
to the beach in winter. Her tiny hands
are pink, and he has forgotten her
gloves. Icicles grow from the railing
holding the lake back. He hands
one to her; it is as tall as she is.
They walk along the beach, still holding
icicles though their hands ache. It is only
the two of them, and the sky comes in close
to snow them out. Watch them walk back
to the car together. Once, she trips, almost falls,
and his hand flutters at his side.

Zombie Dad

Years before he will leave
my dad comes for me
in the night. In the hallway,
arms outstretched,
he staggers forward
playing monster.
The wild shriek
of his daughter
a lure that draws him
ever nearer. It is as if
my scream—half laugh,
half shrill clarion of fear,
manifests this father.
I create him,
and just like any
of the other minor gods,
lose control of my making.
His eyes half-lidded &
his arms open,
he steps blindly
into the future
dark
& feels around
for the switch.

Some Brief Information about the Spartans

after Mestrius Plutarch

In back rooms, boys tend their dying fathers like gardens.
They fold the fathers' hands into blankets, wrapping
their desiccated limbs like bouquets.

Boys plot the deaths of their fathers, knowing the end
of their fathers is the end of their own futures.

Boys pay tribute to Saint Jude: patron saint of dollar single
cigarettes from the bar, patron saint of working a double
at the granite factory, patron saint of watching
the bitter candle of your father go to hell.

Boys slick their hair, ride their cars up and down, and yell
lewd words to anyone who looks like she might be able to
resist them.

Boys turn their faces to one another to offer up their beauty,
a prize to be hit, again and again until the fruit bruises.

Boys get alcoholic skinny. Their limbs knock around
in their clothes like skinny pines, the flesh of their bodies fine
and preserved in brine. Still their beauty flickers
in their faces, cuts at any who can stand to look.

Boys turn to men, after a shift, slicking back their long hair.
Pretty as a girl. Irrigating the soil of their skin with their
fathers' cologne, they tuck in their shirts. Enter the night
as a lighthouse enters the fog.

Boys get heroin skinny. Cheekbones stand up in relief
from the maps of their faces. Boys begin to hoard their teeth
like arcade coins. They use their beauty to lure death closer.

A boy wants a woman who will mourn him.

A boy laughs, and it scares all who hear. It is a train whistle at
2:00 a.m. It is the sound of a struck dog begging to die.
It will inhabit you if you agree to host.

A boy prowls his prison cell with the grief and grace
of a ballerina.

In prison, a boy begins to cultivate his muscles like hothouse
flowers. They are the only beauty he has left. They bloom,
fragrant, glistening.

In prison, a boy works in the greenhouse for thirty-five cents
an hour. In this way, captivity becomes a learned art.
This is called a life skill.

In prison, a boy plants a wedding ring, hoping it will grow
into a life raft.

Each week, in prison, a woman comes to the boy to weep
over him. In fear, he cannot touch her. She is the altar
where he's laid his life.

A boy gets out of prison to find that the world he loves plots
his gruesome end.

Boys throw great parties in celebration of their impending doom. They compete to attain great oblivion. This oblivion has many names: forget me; hit me; let me drink great quantities of clear, evil liquor; let me throw my body into yours until we are nothing; fast, lovely machine; a lover's violent death; my violent death where and when I choose to die, and not before, fuckers.

In the dark, boys lie on their beds and listen to the katydids and frogs wetly hum. So, too, they hum. A bat whines. A boy thinks of all that he will kill. All that will try to kill him.

Homecoming

Somewhere in Illinois, my uncle is trying,
very sincerely, to die & divest himself of his body.

When he succeeds, the locks of the dam will yield
to allow whatever is in there to flow out. What release.

What give. What expanse of green water flung away
from itself to tumble, joyous, into nothing.

When you and I were nineteen and drunk,
you used to play music in the dark, music

we'd clutch each other to, music you used
to guide you to the cliff of unconsciousness.

Jason Molina & Low & Sigur Rós & Nina Simone,
songs I swore to you I couldn't remember, but today

I listened to "Farewell Transmission" and I knew all
the words, every twang of the dirty guitar
and the defiant panic

of Jason Molina wailing about midnight, that carnivore,
ripping the moon's soft body to shreds, the train of sleep

bearing down on him all the while, and somehow
despite the drunkenness, despite our inert
sleep-sodden forms

spiraling off into our separate, twinned nothings,
I know the grief, I know the song,
I could sing it in my sleep. How does my body do it?

Hum with a song past all knowing, past all desire?

Somewhere, someone relaxes into oblivion,
each muscle unlocking each body, each body

singing O, the thunder, the train, the wet cloak
of dark descends, the undertow & the crows fling

themselves from the tree, smear of pitch, little infinity
of unending echo, his mouth hung open as if about to sing.

Quitting the Pack

One Spartan mother saw her son in the distance, panting and in
tears as he returned home from battle.
    She called out to the boy, "How did we do there, my son?"
The boy called back, crying, "All my friends are dead, mom!"
The mother picked up a stone and then hurled it at her son.
He was struck in the head and died there in the road.
"May they forgive you, then, for your treachery."
*Some Information about the Spartans, Mestrius Plutarch, trans. John
    D'Agata*

A boy quits the pack to devote more time
to his wounds. He holds them

to himself, keeping inventory of his pain.
At night he risks a glance to let them breathe in the air.

Jewel-toned, they glister wetly, gasp.

His retirement fund, dear mouths, his dowry,
his *hello goodbyes*, his only possessions.

————

We must look at his death, welcome it
hello goodbye

we love him, we want to look away,
we want him to let us be.

He gathers his wounds to him,
the last of his art.

Do not ask, *Is this the only thing he has made?*

We will watch him make it to the last;

he has been rehearsing fifty years.
Look, he gathers his wounds to himself,

a last little light to read by.

———

We must make one last metaphor to carry him

a small warm creature runs out
of the cage of his chest
and into the mouth of the oblivious sky,
void without end

———

Now desiccated and small, all
the juice wrung out and whatever

loveliness evaporated, distilled
so we have to peer down

the long black well of him
to see it,

small silent pool at his center.

hello goodbye

How They Die

We heard it was an accident, but his mother says different.

They drink themselves until their persons unravel.

Homeless, on the beach, doing ice.

Shot.

In other countries, screaming.

They go mad and we forget them.

They hang themselves.

Wild.

Alone, or in the house of some other sickened father.

Often and in numbers too many to count.

They go into a tunnel and never come out.

hum

A father sleeps alone,
his hands finally relaxed

like old worn socks at day's end.
In his dream he is just a fatherless boy

swimming in a bottomless lake.
The lake has no borders. In his dream

he is trapped in the space of the lake—
it is his whole world, and he begins to suffocate.

                Suddenly, he wakes.
The curtains in the dusky bedroom
can't muffle the hum of the neon street.

Jobs

(The one where you were a carpenter)
Eight hours of the saw, electric,
and your hands dream
of the silver spin,
the cut,
pine and skin.

Everything you could make.
Everything that could unmake you.

(The one in the Mitsubishi plant)
You, made of tin,
thin as a violin string,
going where the union man won't.

The belly of the smoke-
stacks. A length of time
unclocked. Black close
as close fog. Imagine
the sudden arm
that finds you.

(The one in the greenhouse)
Repetition patterns
what's quilted on closed eyelids:
rows of posies,
rows of posies,
rows of posies.

Dirt ground
into furrowed hand.

(The one where you hauled granite)
A joke about Sisyphus: body
without self. Bowed
body strung bow-taut.

(The one where you counted soybeans)
Hill of beanscounter:

Everyone can amount
to something.

(The one at the lumberyard)
Storm spins out,
spiral widening the sky.

Hazard new hands given forklifts,
hazard the levers, hazard
the hounding rain.

(The one in the chemical plant)
Into the drum
the turbine moves you:

Here, everyone knows someone
dead.

(After hours)
Eat an orange and
it's gone but for

the zest flesh
under the rind
of your nail,
the stinging smell,
the slow peel
going to seed.

Some Boys of the Midwest

after Ben Marcus

Boys court me. We leave the restaurant, where they sat
uncomfortable and did not know where to put their elbows.
Shyly they take my hand to help me into the car. Shyly they
part the sea of empty Mountain Dew cans in the back seat
and reach for me, leave their bites all over me. The boys are
unwashed and smell like food—as if they have been lightly
battered and fried in their own grease. The boys hold my
hands in theirs until they begin to ache. The parking lot
empties, leaving a vast ocean of tar under yellow light. It
is five in the morning. A wild red fox streaks past the car,
something wriggling in his mouth. Even in the dark, it is easy
to tell who consumes who.

After we have fucked & you turn into a horse

After we have fucked & you turn into a horse
you are curled in the center of the bed, gentled

& I can run my hand down your flank & you
smell of sweet horse & hay & manure

& nature seems to cloak you in her moss
& though you are at rest, your hot muscles tremble

& it looks as though you could break
into a sprint & so to run my hand along your flank

& so to run my small hot hand along
the plane of your flank & so to run my long

pale hand along your flank & maybe to lick
the sweat from your horse

-body is a danger, as it is dangerous when any
domesticated animal encounters a wild one

& when you turn, little horse, into my hand as I pet
you, seeking the patch of sun that is my hand

gentling you, that hot bitter pride rises up in me,

that you are my horse:

& that is why
I must kill you & suck clean the bones.

three

But how do you choose your form? How do you choose your name? How do you choose your life?

—JOANNA NEWSOM, "DIVERS"

A Nightmare Is a Body and Your Father Gone

A nightmare is a Body and your father gone,
& time is the road you travel to him.

& in the Body clocks all stopped & in the Body
time unclocked & "doing time"—the father does it

& you—the Body—do it too. The Body is heavy
now with time, with all the stories told of time:

"It's not so long" & "Don't forget" &—sweetest—
"there will still be time," those myths against

time's length & memory & grief.
The father's body clocks his time

in letters, in lost hair, lost teeth, in muscle gained &
places secret, unseen, unknown and loved—

the Body holds its time inside, an organ called
the gonefather: that little velvet pocket & a cloud

cast on the heart. You don't know how
to say it but the Body can, it must,

Body clinging to the bodies of the Uncles,
those fathers of children not-you.

Sweet brittle persistent body,

clutching the father's artifacts & dust,
eating the father's letters until sick with glut.

Body, your very composition is an absence
& lay you down to sleep in his T-shirts

& be now the child & be the father both
& hold your little self & hold the gonefather

at your center & make of it a timeless world:
throw up your firmament of eternal tears.

The lack at the heart of you is your making, the lack
at the heart of you is where you learn to make.

Good Girl

A man with his hands in my mouth
asked me was I okay. Was I feeling it?
Was I going to do anything
this weekend?
Underneath the drilling
my mouth alternately
roiled a blood-pink froth
and lay dormant,
its little animal will
silent and watchful.

The blue silicone really is the best,
said the man to the woman
who held the implements.
Let's use the blue from now on,
said the man. *Katie,* he said
(his hands tending
my little garden of rot),
what do you prefer?
Katie or Kate? Katie you are
so patient, thank you, you are
so patient. And I lay in the chair
holding my smile.

Nowhere

I left work
and walked down Prospect
past the Long John Silver's,
the Mexican place, the Jiffy
Lube, the gas station, the liquor store
where, in the parking lot, a man
held his woman by the wrist
and steered her into the frigid
bounty of the shop. She could
barely stand. She sprawled,
belly down on the counter, laughing.
At the light a man rode up
on a bike and looked me up
then down. *Baby my car's*
in the shop, but if it wasn't
I would take you anywhere
you wanted to go. I thought
of the gas station, the cold
of it, the fluorescent donuts
in their case, the rows
of colorful, flavored gums
with heavenly names.
I once walked in there
to buy a pack of gum
and stayed for an hour.
The impossible choice.
The mango pineapple oasis,
the waterberry splash.
The cool-mint melondream
breeze. So I jumped on the handlebars.
Down Prospect, the fast food
joints just fast rainbows now,

I could see the way cumulus
clouds of fry grease hung above
the places like the threat of a storm.
Faster and faster now, the trees whipping
by in a fury of green. The city,
the highway, the exhale of farms.
Orange sun setting like a sick egg.
And into another state altogether.
No one knows us here, he said,
and I held him tighter while we ghosted
slowly through humid neighborhoods,
warped houses that teemed
with dead cars, with guinea pig
colonies, with wan families
and their mashed-potato dinners.
We set up home. We made Wednesday
night spaghetti night. He rode
his bike for pay, and in the mornings
out back I tended to the guinea pigs,
their bodies moving through
the high grass like tiny housecats
stalking their prey. They were untame,
majestic. They were a horde of mouths
under the house. At dawn I saw them
teeming the ceiling. They'd scatter
like bugs when I got a glass of water
in the kitchen. They were dear to me.
And then one day the wind came
in the house. Nothing stayed put.
The papers, the pigs, the furniture began
to beat at me. Tornadoes in the kitchen,
tornadoes of fur and plates.

We have to leave, I said. *The wind*
is in the house. The wind is
the house. Everything is wild
and cruel. So he got his bike.
Past the grey houses, the cold lawns,
the dead cars, the wan little girls chalking
up the street. The pigs fanned out
behind us, a furry retinue. But in the end
they flagged. Short legs.
Past the city limits, the moneyed suburbs,
the miles and miles of inedible corn.
Where are we going now, he said. *Nowhere,*
I said. *They're still behind us,* I said.
Keep going, I said. *Faster, faster.*
It's going to be great. It's going to be
like nothing you've ever seen.

The Spouse

The one whose cubbyhole—whose rodent burrow—nears
your own. The spouse scatters when the light is flipped. The
spouse requires darkness and a little nest fluff—that's all.
It's true: the spouse can be a pest. Spouses have overrun the
neighborhood. The neighborhood watch will outline a plan
to eliminate spouses at the next neighborhood association
meeting. Attendance at the meeting discussing spousal
extermination is mandatory. You will be required to pay
for the removal of your own spouse infestation. Consider a
bake sale, a Patreon account, a Kickstarter. There are many
modern ways for an intrepid, thrifty homeowner to raise
money for spouse removal. Remember that spouses look
small and idiotic, but their deviant skills are vast. They breed
in such numbers! How to recognize a spouse: it is *a strange
object covered in fur which breaks your heart*. It is a houseguest
you found charming who now refuses to leave. You may
have unknowingly cuddled the spouse; check yourself for
infection. A spouse is a technology of rubbing that becomes
a habit. In the daytime, the spouse goes back to wherever
it does its diurnal business. It's almost too disgusting to
be believed. Nothing that has ever been clean has been a
spouse.

Portrait of Womb, Mixed Media

Twenty-nine-year-old womb as little sleeping bag & wolf-
at-door; as ocean cave with soft anemone; no,

as shuddery song of an unseen whale,
you know it lives, not where and how.

Womb as dance hall and everyone's left
but the drunk piano man who weeps into

his beer, rallies a little, tries to plink out a tune.
Drunk womb, limping limply. Womb as headline:

LOCAL WOMB TRIES TO CREATE HUMAN, MANIFESTS
SINGLE CREEPY LITTLE GHOST. Womb as businessman,

examining himself for quarterly returns.
Womb as hard-boiled egg, peeled: small moon

of a thin fingernail to remove the shell and silk
membrane, sulfurous release, gelatin wet white

and the fur and velvet of yolk unyolked. Consumed.
Womb as death-of-dream; as birth of death;

as crabgrass chewed into evil milk
and a little hiccup to help it down.

Self-portrait of womb as answered question.
Self-portrait of womb with baby as gun.

Body Lessons

I never liked being in here, the broad injustice of the body,
of being shoved back down into it, just when I knew I could

take leave of it, come up out of it and unfurl like smoke
from a hot grill. But you shoved me back into it and I'm

not mad, we're here together and you're doing your thing:
multiplying furiously—your first art project: knitting yourself

together out of nothing, trawling the outer reaches of space
with a net full of stars like a fisherman,
bringing in some dust bunnies

that an errant, dirty god was too careless to clean up.
That is how you make your body:
from the leftovers in the corners of celestial refrigerators.

It is good to watch you take the leavings and make yourself.
It is good that you are here with me, and I can cast

my ear to my sonic depths like a whale and ask you,
Are you here? and listen to your raw little voice reply,
I'm mine I'm mine I'm mine.

The Island of Lost Things

The nurse searches the taut globe of my stomach, sounding
its depths for the heartbeat. The ease with which I long for her

to hear it is a sign of my weakness. On an island somewhere,
my grandmother's wedding rings roll along, finally sentient

after their fifty-year orbit on the planetary axis of her finger,
the five-year orbit on mine. The gold worn thin as hard candy

that has been worried and sucked to translucence. The book
I read or meant to read and lent to an acquaintance I longed

to impress with my erudition huddles next to the fire, plays
the harmonica with a melancholy air. And in a tree, a baby girl

lights on a branch, perches, tucks her head
between her shoulder blades, and falls asleep, falls out of the tree,
falls out of her own life.

I never heard her song. I long to hear it now.
It is not given to me to hear it.

At home, I go from room to room, searching. The curtains
in the bedroom hang in awful stasis. *What is wrong with you*

that you must worry the space where the tooth once was, that pain
that is an itch, until blood rises to greet your fretting? Somehow

the pain demands an answer. I hurry to answer it. I hurry
as if there is an answer. As if the want of an answer is not itself
the answer.

I long to place the girl who is a failed bird back into the tree.
The rings back on a finger. The book on its shelf.
It is wrong to want

the impossible, to continue wanting, as if the wanting
is an action, and besides, the lost things are alive now,
as if the state of being lost

has breathed blood and health into their frames.
The nurse sounds the depths of my stomach
as if it were an ocean,

as if the island is hard to find, though I feel it
rise under my skin. In this moment before elation
or disaster, I've lived my whole life.

After the Miscarriage

I
The stream is a strip of late-August gold,
and the dog's gone on ahead, snuffling

up and down the moss, so green it trembles,
her nose throbbing in that live carpet,

two wet creatures running their lengths
along each other. And then

the dog lunges, snaps her jaw—

and the bird unfolds its wings, no,
a moth unfolds its wings against her mouth.

It shudders on the bank. Before I end it,
I have to touch it so that it knows I live.

Horror in the jaws that snatch you down.
Horror in not knowing your killer.

II
Its wings are too burdensome for its body, so that it looks
painful. Two eyes mark them, so that it seems to stare,

and where I've stomped on them, the wings are torn
and dirty as old sheets that you'd meant to keep nice.

Their lifespans are short: a large silk moth
lives only a week, sticky invisible thread stretching

birth to death, and its mouth useless, vestigial,

the hinges creaking as the hinges of kitchen doors do,

revealing the empty room within. Something so delicate
cannot live very long unsoiled.

III
The doctor sounds for the larval blip.
In the moment before she tells me you're dead,

eternity opens. I live in the space where your heartbeat
should be. I see your tissue paper lungs filling with fluid.

My body echoes in its dark chamber; only witness
to a body no one will see. No one will mourn.

What do you want to do? the doctor says.
Get it out, I say. This is the last time I mother you.

IV
The moth is named *polyphemus* for the monster
blinded by Odysseus. *Who is it that wounds me?*

the monster cried, and Odysseus said, *My name
is nobody,* and the monster hung his grief

like curtains in the air, and his family rushed to him,
crying, *Who has wounded you thus?* and Polyphemus

replied, *Nobody nobody no body no body no body*—
his story ends here. In some stories, the injured is gifted

oblivion, falling out of memory like a bird
from a nest, and the story moves on without him.

Odysseus must continue—must strap himself
to the mast and beg to be flung into the water,

must eat, must fuck, must wander to the end
of the story and tell it, too. Horror of the killer.

Error

for Sarah, for Jill, for Jen

In the backyard, a group of women huddles
over the corpse of a woman. This is incorrect.

Do they seek its heat, her body's flame of decomposition?
Or do they wait for her body to flower?

When the body makes something dead—for instance,
when a womb produces vats upon vats of hot orange marmalade—

how should one proceed in the face of such error?

There are those who might ignore the error, politely
turning away and averting their eyes. How else

to reject the bad luck that perfumes the one who is wrong?
It will infect those who look on it. Then there are those

other, those rare: they gather their jars and begin
to bottle the error. They produce the fire and hold

their bread up to it, they spread the error over the toast
and remark upon its coloring, its flavor, the bitterness

of the rind. They eat it; they know its weight and heft.
Look, they say to the wrong one, *look how we bear it.*

It is summer so my cunt wears me

like a human hat and I trail behind it,

sincere and embarrassed for us.
The city fills up with bickering cunt

like the elderly flooding a matinee
or a Denny's, cunt swamps the natural

topography, and everyone goes bonkers.
A thousand men in vans glide past girls on the street

and, opening the sliding doors, lean out to tell
them how the weather system of their cunts

affects the world. Like a thousand Bukowskis
they list their own special skills in cunting,

the spelunking tools they've purchased
at great expense. They claim a fever, they claim

whatever they can get. A girl rattling her cage
manages, in the wee hours of the morning—

through elaborate rituals involving
feminine douche—to detach

her cunt, and the cunt marches purposefully
away into the night (probably to make

a go of it in the wilderness, but who knows).
The girl looks after the retreating form

of the cunt and thinks fondly of it now
that she can abstract it. Thinks of the cunt

as an alien creature she was in thrall to,
then thinks guiltily of the movie *Her*

and wonders if the cunt *wanted* to get away?
To be with its own kind? At work, *eau d'cunt*

drifts up around me, my cunt mouthing off,
and I go to the bathroom to piss, and there

in the corner of the stall a giant cockroach glossy
and dead lies belly up. My cunt hiccups my cunt mourns it

animal to animal, the body reviled   the body
that was not big enough to contain it, whatever it was.

After the Hospital

He took me to the Big Fancy, that grocery store
where illusion backlights the dairy case & everything

pulses with blue light. I shuffled the store, still unsteady,
still in my pajamas. In the snack aisle, one thousand kinds

of chips, all so beautiful, shiny & wet. I had insisted
that I be able to get whatever I wanted after the procedure.

Still groggy from the anesthesia they had used to get inside
me, to cut it out, the olive bar seemed obscene the longer

I stared at it: many wet nodes! wet eyes! Everything in here
glistens. I should be able to have anything, anything I want.

Where is it? My hospital band means *absence.* It collars
my wrist where I am a dog to my lack.

What it's like to touch the girl
you've been longing to touch

She lays her hands on you.
Don't call it burning, stupid.

You'll have to invent a new metaphor:
her hands are on you   where

she touches, flutes spring
from your body.

It's a little painful, this woodwind
section of your body,

breathing   making honking noises.
It's a little fucking corny

this singing, unsettling orchestra
tuning itself under her hands, preening—

How to decide if you want to wear her
clothes, or straddle her and lick them off.

The fugue that comes out of you stutters
and repeats   is that squawking

music, or pain? *both, both*, little sousaphone,
        neither horn nor bird.

In kindergarten you held your best friend
or, at least, her hand   and felt a creature stir

in your chest when she looked at someone
else. You crushed her hand in yours,

the creature crowing possessive.
What was it
        you wanted from her?

Only to cease the endless separation between you,
only to end selfhood once and for all,

crossing into each other, abolishing all nationhood.
The creature in your chest stood, ruffling his feathers,

turned once, and with a cry, grew the hollow cavity
required of all animals who make that violent music

and call it love.

The Horse in the Field

Outside my apartment
the border of the yard ends
in the alley and the alley
goes to the street
and the street will go
past many homes whose
interiors flare with a blue
light and the street will go
past the parks filled with
decorative lakes stocked
with heavy jeweled koi
in their eternal decorative
swim and at the end of the street
there is a field and in the field
there is a very tiny horse.

The horse is new and stands
like she just learned how,
but her eyes are old and alien
and blue. She looks as though
her hair is fine and soft. She looks
as though she was made to be
a fine little object. But she is just
a tiny horse in a field.

                    In my house I move from room
                    to room. I take the dumbbells
                    from their place in the bathroom
                    and do many repetitive movements.
                    I examine my belly to see if it looks
                    concave when I lie down,
                    as a girl once told me it should.

Meanwhile, the horse is in the field.
The horse is tiny but has acquired mass.
A floodlight is on the horse, illuminating
her for all to see. Many people
come to look at the horse. The horse
looks back. The horse's fur seems
to obscurely question their way of life.
The people wonder what is the meaning
of the horse's fur. Preachers are sent for.

I can't decide what to eat for dinner.
I look on the internet for what to eat for dinner.
Charlene has posted a soup that looks
almost pornographic. I look in my crisper
drawer, but there's just a few carrots,
growing old and hairy, hysterical
in their claustrophobia.

In the field, the horse seems to be giving
off light and heat. The preachers have
begun their sermons, and the people listen
to the meaning of the horse. They sing
and weep in the field. They erect tents.

A fringe group of herbalists
stands outside the tents, hawking a formula
constructed of horse hoof clippings and said to cure
impotence of all kinds. The horse's delicate ears
extend from her head as if reaching
into the night and testing for safety.

I spend all evening scrubbing baseboards
and arranging my clothing according to sleeve length.
Some supplicants have shown up at my door
on their way to the field. They ask for food
and I give them the carrots, a few oranges,
a little milk and a half box of Junior Mints.

One asks for a blessing and I do my best:
There's traffic on 14th, I say. *May it always
be so,* the supplicant responds.

At the field, horse interpretation
gets to be a thing, with local meteorologists
standing as close as they dare and interpreting
the horse markings to the growing crowds.
One says the horse tells us about time.
The other says the horse tells us about loss.
A third rebukes the first and claims the horse
is atemporal. The horse's snout makes a snuffle
that has everyone taking out their phones
and hitting record.

The supplicants have started to camp on my porch.
There's a rumor that I know the horse.
I try to explain that I know the fact of the horse
but nothing else. They don't believe me.
From across the porch, one has made a nest
of Hostess wrappers. From deep within his nest, he begins
to shoot me glances I don't know how to interpret.
I get the sense someone's agitating, but I
only hear whispers when I turn my back.

In the field, the horse has begun to lose her looks.
It looks like an old trash bag, the people lament.
People begin to throw stuff at the horse,
shoes and apples, handfuls of grass, and tracts
about the horse that someone printed in town.
Beautiful thing horse! the tracts say.
It means the world to us!

The agitator from the porch drags me
to the field to confront my knowledge
of the horse. They invite me to make a speech.

I don't know what to say, I say.

What does it mean if it's not beautiful? someone shouts.

I know the horse has put her beauty away for a reason.
I know the horse won't tell me why. The horse
couldn't tell if she wanted to. If she could want.

In the field, the horse begins to shed her skin,
a thing I wasn't aware horses could do.
The horse's ugliness increases.
People begin throwing out insults to see
which one they all like the best. *The horse
looks like an old sofa you'd take
to the curb. The horse looks like a trash fire, like a dog
made out of diapers, like a hairy
lollipop. The horse looks like an exposed wound.*

In all the confusion, the horse has retreated
to the edge of the field. There is a slight shimmer
at the edge, and darkness beyond. I have time
to build a fantasy about joining the horse:
standing in the field, the fog rolling off the night
grass and encircling our bodies.
The image flares like a candle in my chest
and then they are on me.

Apple Glory

In my front yard a man in a bulldozer has dug a grave.
They say it's for a fire hydrant. It looks sepulchral—

a ladder descends into the earth as if you could take the
stairs right to hell. Last night a collared tabby appeared

out of the sewer and circled the hole. I want to tell you
how brave she looked, sitting on the lip of the abyss.

I want, like the cat, to know what eternity smells like.
She wore a collar around her neck. Maybe it felt like prison.

Maybe it felt like a blessing tethering her to an Earth she'd
like, for one ecstatic moment, to leave. For now, death is

our only access to the multiverse, and a man I know got to go
this morning. He was not a nice man. At the end, he did not

believe he would die, though perhaps he felt his body slowly
sloughing itself off, soft mask. I don't know how to mourn

a cruel man. Though I reach for it, all my beauty deserts me,
my wings do not unfold. I cook thinly sliced apples in butter.

I beat eggs. There are very few transformations allowed, here.
This is one. Glory. Some men cannot give themselves

to life. Glory. These men are the most reluctant to die. Glory.
I sit at the lip of the abyss. I can smell it. Glory, glory.

The Daughter

I found a dead cricket in my underwear,
its arms splayed like a sleeping baby,

and I knew I'd birthed it—my sleeping body
had churned out this angelic dead

made from dreaming & the froth
the body makes when it is denied what it longs for most.

The craving had made a dead thing.

The cricket had the face of my daughter—
a face no one will see. Because I wanted her,

I held my daughter (her ancient
verdigris face) & then I swallowed her whole.

acknowledgments

Without readings and rereadings by Kwame Dawes, Emily Skaja, David Henson, Ángel García, and Katie Marya, this book would not exist. All errors are mine. What is true here has been overseen and tenderly corrected by many thoughtful hands.

In 2011 Beth Loffreda asked me a question about the narratives of masculinity in my poetry that altered the course of this book. Claudia Rankine's workshop on long forms changed what I thought the landscape of a poem could do, and though it took me several months after the class was over to write "Daughter Psalms," that poem would not have existed without Claudia Rankine's brilliance. The incisive teaching, kindness, and editorial eye of Kate Northrop, Brad Watson, Grace Bauer, Stacey Waite, and Ted Kooser have been instrumental, as has early encouragement from Carmella Braniger, Stephen Frech, Chuck Rybak, and Jan Zwicky.

Thank you to my cohort at the University of Wyoming MFA, and to my cohort at the University of Nebraska, Lincoln, PhD. Special thanks to Scott Pinkmountain, Maya Cohen, Kristen Gunther, Emily Trostel, and Ryler Dustin, who read early versions of this book and gave me thoughtful notes and encouragement.

Thank you to the team at the University of New Mexico Press, especially Elise McHugh and James Ayers for their compassionate, keen editorial minds, and for gently walking me through this process.

To my family, the Schmids: possessed of a preternatural intelligence and storytelling so incisive and hilarious I have spent my whole life trying to keep up. To my family, the Clarks: for being the most self-effacing, kind people I know. To my family, the Hensons: gifted with warmth and

wisdom and a secret iconoclastic streak. To my mother-
and father-in-law, Mary Kay and Brian. To my mom, Pat.
My dad, Shawn. My stepmom, Dotty.

Thank you to Anne Gilligan. I know you would insist
that I did most of the work of walking myself home from
hell, but it's always nice to have a companion who knows
the way.

To Colleen Cunningham, to Stephanie Williams-
Purdom. To Josh Wild. To Emily Skaja, again. To David,
my first reader, my first love, my biggest co-conspirator.
To Margot, who tells me often that she is a better poet
than me, and who is right.

Grateful acknowledgement is made to the journals in
which these poems first appeared, sometimes in earlier
forms:

American Literary Review: "Apple Glory"
Best New Poets 2009: "Jobs"
Booth: a journal: "The Spouse" and "Portrait of Womb:
    Mixed Media"
decomP: "After the Hospital"
Hobart: "Nowhere" and "In the Gothic Love Story
    Where You Have Died"
Pank: "The Boys of the Midwest, 1–5"
The Pinch: "What it's like to touch the girl you've been
    longing to touch"
Third Point Press: "A Nightmare Is a Body and Your
    Father Gone"
Quarterly West: "Daughter Psalms" and "hum"
Redivider: "At the Bus Stop"
Sixth Finch: "The Horse in the Field"
The Southeast Review: "At their first meeting . . ."

Southern Indiana Review: "Writing to my Father in
   Prison" and "Zombie Father"
The Spectacle: "All my Boyfriends Love my Father the
   Best" and "How they Die"
Under a Warm Green Linden: "Loving an Addict"

The following poems appeared in the chapbook *Forget
Me, Hit Me, Let Me Drink Great Quantities of Clear, Evil
Liquor,* from Split Lip Press:

"Boys of the Midwest"
"Daughter Psalms"
"Homecoming"
"Jobs"
"Nowhere"
"Some Brief Information about the Spartans"

notes

The first epigraph is from Selah Saterstrom's *Ideal Suggestions: Essays in Divinatory Poetics*, published by Essay Press in 2017. Thank you to Selah for allowing me to excerpt it here.

"The Boys of the Midwest" series is in conversation with Ben Marcus's *The Age of Wire and String*. It has been over ten years since I read the book, but the prose poems in it struck me, at the time, as being containers for grief.

The second epigraph appears with thanks to Ian Daly and his Aunt Michele for use of an excerpt from Jeffrey Miller's letters. I encountered Miller's letters in the article "You Can't Come Halfway Home from the Bar," published on the Poetry Foundation website on December 17, 2008.

"Some Brief Information about the Spartans" is inspired by and "Quitting the Pack" has an epigraph from John D'Agata's translation of Mestrius Plutarch's "Some Information About the Spartans," which appears in his book *The Lost Origins of the Essay*, published by Graywolf Press in 2009. Thank you to John for allowing me to excerpt it here.

The final epigraph is a line from Joanna Newsom that appears on her album *Divers*, released by Drag City in 2015.

"The Spouse" contains the perfect line "a strange object covered in fur which breaks your heart" by Donald Barthelme, from his out of print short story collection *Come Back, Dr. Caligari*, published in 1971 by Little, Brown & Co.